EMMANUEL JOSEPH

The Soundtrack of Humanity, Music, Mind, and the Tapestry of Human History

Copyright © 2025 by Emmanuel Joseph

All rights reserved. No part of this publication may be reproduced, stored or transmitted in any form or by any means, electronic, mechanical, photocopying, recording, scanning, or otherwise without written permission from the publisher. It is illegal to copy this book, post it to a website, or distribute it by any other means without permission.

First edition

*This book was professionally typeset on Reedsy.
Find out more at reedsy.com*

Contents

1	Chapter 1: The Dawn of Music	1
2	Chapter 2: The Power of Melody and Harmony	3
3	Chapter 3: Rhythm and the Human Pulse	5
4	Chapter 4: The Evolution of Musical Instruments	7
5	Chapter 5: Music and Emotion	9
6	Chapter 6: Music and Memory	11
7	Chapter 7: Music and Identity	13
8	Chapter 8: The Healing Power of Music	15
9	Chapter 9: Music and Technology	17
10	Chapter 10: Music and Culture	19
11	Chapter 11: The Future of Music	21
12	Chapter 12: The Universal Language of Music	23
13	Chapter 13: Music in Times of Crisis	25
14	Chapter 14: The Global Soundtrack	27

1

Chapter 1: The Dawn of Music

Music's roots lie deep in the history of humanity, predating even written language. Ancient civilizations employed music as a means of communication, a tool for social cohesion, and a method to connect with the divine. Early humans used rudimentary instruments like drums and flutes made from bones, which evolved over millennia into the sophisticated instruments we know today. This chapter explores the earliest forms of music, their purpose, and their evolution through various ancient cultures.

We delve into the mesmerizing rhythm of tribal drums echoing through dense forests, the haunting melodies of flutes resonating in ancient caves, and the chanted hymns that reverberated within the sacred walls of temples. Each beat, each note, each song tells a story, weaving a rich tapestry of human experience and emotion. The chapter also sheds light on the archaeological discoveries that have given us a glimpse into the musical practices of our ancestors, illuminating the universality and timelessness of music.

Furthermore, we investigate the role of music in ancient rituals and ceremonies, where it served as a bridge between the mortal and the divine. From the intricate soundscapes of ancient Egypt to the rhythmic complexities of African tribal music, we explore how music was used to celebrate life, mourn death, and everything in between. Music was not merely an art form; it was an essential component of the human experience, deeply interwoven with the cultural and spiritual fabric of society.

Finally, we examine the cognitive and emotional impact of early music on the human mind. How did these primitive sounds influence the development of the human brain, and how did they shape our ancestors' perceptions of the world around them? Through this exploration, we begin to understand the profound connection between music, mind, and the human spirit.

2

Chapter 2: The Power of Melody and Harmony

In this chapter, we delve into the fundamental building blocks of music: melody and harmony. The exploration begins with the definition and distinction between these two elements, followed by an analysis of their roles in various musical traditions across the globe. Melodies have the power to evoke emotions and create memorable musical phrases, while harmonies add depth and richness to these melodies, creating a more complex and satisfying auditory experience.

We trace the development of melody and harmony from their early use in folk music to their sophisticated application in classical compositions. The chapter highlights key milestones in musical history, such as the invention of polyphony in medieval Europe, which marked a significant leap in the complexity and texture of music. This innovation allowed multiple independent melodies to be sung or played simultaneously, creating a rich tapestry of sound that was previously unheard.

The chapter also explores the psychological effects of melody and harmony on the human brain. Why do certain melodies stick in our minds, and how do harmonies enhance our emotional response to music? By examining studies in music psychology and neuroscience, we gain insight into the ways in which our brains process and respond to these fundamental musical elements. This understanding underscores the powerful impact that melody and harmony can have on our emotions and memories.

Additionally, we look at the cultural significance of melody and harmony in different societies. From the intricate ragas of Indian classical music to the harmonious choral traditions of European cathedrals, we see how these elements are woven into the fabric of cultural identity. Music serves not only as entertainment but also as a means of expressing cultural values, beliefs, and histories, reinforcing the idea that the soundtrack of humanity is as diverse and multifaceted as humanity itself.

3

Chapter 3: Rhythm and the Human Pulse

Rhythm is the heartbeat of music, an elemental force that drives the tempo and structure of a piece. This chapter explores the significance of rhythm in various musical genres and its impact on human cognition and emotion. We begin by defining rhythm and its components, such as beat, tempo, and meter, and then examine how different cultures utilize rhythm to create distinct musical styles.

We explore the role of rhythm in traditional African drumming, where complex polyrhythms create intricate and mesmerizing patterns. These rhythms are not only a form of musical expression but also serve as a means of communication and social cohesion within communities. The chapter also delves into the syncopated rhythms of jazz, the driving beats of rock and roll, and the pulsating electronic rhythms of modern dance music, showcasing the versatility and universality of rhythm.

The chapter highlights the connection between rhythm and the human body, particularly the way rhythmic patterns can influence our physical responses. From the instinctive urge to tap our feet to the beat to the therapeutic effects of rhythmic drumming in music therapy, we explore how rhythm resonates with our biological rhythms and affects our mood and behavior. This connection underscores the profound impact that rhythm can have on our overall well-being.

We also examine the role of rhythm in the brain, exploring how different rhythmic patterns can affect brain activity and cognitive processes. Studies in music therapy and neuroscience have shown that rhythmic stimulation can improve motor skills, enhance memory, and even alleviate symptoms of certain neurological disorders. This chapter provides a comprehensive look at the ways in which rhythm shapes our musical experiences and influences our mental and physical health.

4

Chapter 4: The Evolution of Musical Instruments

Musical instruments have evolved alongside human civilization, reflecting the technological advancements and cultural shifts of each era. This chapter traces the history of musical instruments, from the earliest rudimentary tools to the sophisticated electronic instruments of the modern age. We explore the ingenuity and creativity that have driven the development of instruments, as well as the cultural and social contexts in which they emerged.

We begin with an exploration of ancient instruments, such as the bone flutes of the Paleolithic era and the lyres of ancient Mesopotamia. These early instruments were often crafted from natural materials and played a central role in rituals and ceremonies. The chapter also examines the innovations of classical antiquity, including the development of stringed instruments like the kithara and the introduction of brass and woodwind instruments in ancient Greece and Rome.

The chapter then moves on to the medieval and Renaissance periods, where significant advancements in instrument design and manufacturing took place. The invention of the violin, the evolution of keyboard instruments like the harpsichord and clavichord, and the development of early wind instruments like the recorder and the sackbut are all explored in detail. These innovations paved the way for the rich orchestral textures of the Baroque and Classical eras.

In the modern era, we see the rise of electronic instruments and digital technology, which have revolutionized the way music is created and performed. From the invention of the electric guitar and synthesizer to the advent of digital audio workstations, the chapter examines the impact of technology on music production and performance. We also explore the cultural implications of these advancements, including the democratization of music-making and the emergence of new genres and styles.

5

Chapter 5: Music and Emotion

Music has the unique ability to evoke a wide range of emotions, from joy and excitement to sadness and nostalgia. This chapter delves into the complex relationship between music and emotion, exploring how different musical elements and structures can influence our emotional responses. We begin by examining the psychological theories that explain why music has such a powerful emotional impact, including the role of melody, harmony, rhythm, and dynamics.

We explore the concept of musical affect, which refers to the emotional content of a piece of music and how it is perceived by the listener. By analyzing examples from various genres and cultures, we see how composers and performers use musical elements to convey specific emotions and create a sense of narrative. From the heart-wrenching adagios of classical symphonies to the uplifting anthems of pop music, we explore the emotional power of music.

The chapter also examines the role of music in regulating and expressing emotions. Music therapy, for example, uses music to help individuals manage their emotions and improve their mental health. We explore the therapeutic benefits of music, including its ability to reduce stress, alleviate anxiety, and enhance mood. By understanding the emotional impact of music, we gain insight into its potential as a tool for healing and well-being.

Additionally, we look at the cultural and social aspects of music and emotion.

THE SOUNDTRACK OF HUMANITY, MUSIC, MIND, AND THE TAPESTRY OF HUMAN HISTORY

How do different cultures use music to express and manage emotions, and how do these practices reflect their values and beliefs? From the cathartic rituals of indigenous communities to the communal celebrations of modern music festivals, we see how music serves as a means of emotional expression and social connection. This chapter highlights the universal and deeply personal nature of music and its ability to touch the human soul.

6

Chapter 6: Music and Memory

The connection between music and memory is profound and multifaceted. This chapter explores how music can trigger memories, enhance learning, and support cognitive function. We begin by examining the neurological basis of music and memory, including the role of the brain's auditory cortex and hippocampus in processing and storing musical information. By understanding the brain's response to music, we gain insight into the powerful connection between music and memory.

We explore the concept of musical reminiscence, which refers to the way that music can evoke memories of specific events, people, and places. By analyzing examples from various genres and cultures, we see how certain songs and pieces of music become associated with personal and collective memories. From the nostalgic melodies of childhood lullabies to the anthems of social movements, we explore the role of music in shaping our memories and identities.

The chapter also examines the use of music as a tool for enhancing memory and learning. Research in music education and cognitive psychology has shown that music can improve memory retention, enhance language skills, and support cognitive development. We explore the benefits of musical training for children and adults, as well as the potential of music therapy for individuals with memory disorders, such as Alzheimer's disease.

Additionally, we look at the cultural and social aspects of music and memory.

How do different cultures use music to preserve and transmit their histories, traditions, and values? From the oral traditions of indigenous communities to the written scores of classical composers, we see how music serves as a repository of cultural memory. By preserving and transmitting musical knowledge, communities ensure the continuity of their cultural heritage and identity.

Finally, we explore the therapeutic applications of music for individuals with memory disorders. Music therapy has been shown to improve cognitive function and quality of life for individuals with Alzheimer's disease and other forms of dementia. By engaging with familiar music, patients can access long-term memories and enhance their cognitive abilities. This chapter highlights the powerful connection between music and memory and its potential for enhancing our lives.

7

Chapter 7: Music and Identity

Music plays a crucial role in shaping and expressing individual and collective identities. This chapter explores the relationship between music and identity, examining how musical tastes and preferences reflect and influence our sense of self. We begin by exploring the concept of musical identity, which encompasses the ways in which music contributes to our personal and social identities.

We delve into the role of music in adolescence, a period when musical preferences often become closely tied to self-identity. During this formative stage, individuals use music to explore their emotions, assert their independence, and connect with peers. The chapter examines the impact of different genres, subcultures, and musical communities on the development of adolescent identity, highlighting the significance of music in this critical life stage.

The chapter also explores the concept of cultural identity and how music reflects and shapes the identities of different communities. From the traditional folk songs of rural villages to the contemporary hip-hop of urban centers, music serves as a powerful means of expressing cultural values, histories, and experiences. We examine the role of music in social movements and cultural resistance, where it has been used to challenge oppression, assert identity, and promote social change.

Additionally, we look at the ways in which globalization and digital technology have influenced musical identities. The rise of streaming platforms and social media has expanded access to diverse musical genres and enabled the creation of new musical communities. We explore how these developments have influenced individual and collective identities, as well as the ways in which music continues to evolve in a rapidly changing world.

8

Chapter 8: The Healing Power of Music

Music has long been recognized for its therapeutic and healing properties. This chapter delves into the various ways in which music can promote physical, emotional, and mental well-being. We begin by exploring the historical use of music in healing practices, from ancient rituals to modern music therapy. By examining the cultural and historical contexts of these practices, we gain insight into the universal nature of music's healing power.

We explore the physiological effects of music on the body, including its impact on heart rate, blood pressure, and the release of stress hormones. Research has shown that listening to music can reduce stress, alleviate pain, and promote relaxation. We examine the mechanisms behind these effects, including the role of rhythm, melody, and harmony in influencing the body's physiological responses.

The chapter also explores the psychological and emotional benefits of music. Music therapy has been used to treat a wide range of mental health conditions, including depression, anxiety, and post-traumatic stress disorder. By engaging with music, individuals can express their emotions, process trauma, and enhance their overall well-being. We examine case studies and research findings that highlight the effectiveness of music therapy in promoting mental health and emotional resilience.

Additionally, we explore the role of music in social and community healing.

THE SOUNDTRACK OF HUMANITY, MUSIC, MIND, AND THE TAPESTRY OF HUMAN HISTORY

From communal singing in religious ceremonies to music festivals that bring people together, music has the power to foster social connection and create a sense of belonging. We examine the ways in which music can promote social cohesion, support healing after collective trauma, and strengthen community bonds. This chapter highlights the multifaceted and transformative power of music in promoting health and well-being.

9

Chapter 9: Music and Technology

The relationship between music and technology has been a driving force in the evolution of music throughout history. This chapter explores the impact of technological advancements on music creation, production, and consumption. We begin by examining the history of musical technology, from the invention of the first musical instruments to the development of modern digital technology.

We delve into the ways in which technology has revolutionized music production and performance. The invention of recording technology, for example, allowed music to be captured, reproduced, and distributed on a scale never before possible. The chapter also examines the impact of electronic instruments and digital audio workstations on music creation, enabling artists to experiment with new sounds and techniques.

The chapter also explores the influence of technology on music consumption. The rise of streaming platforms, social media, and digital distribution has transformed the way we access and engage with music. We examine the implications of these changes for the music industry, artists, and listeners, as well as the ways in which technology has democratized music-making and expanded access to diverse musical genres.

Additionally, we look at the future of music and technology, exploring emerging trends and innovations. From artificial intelligence and virtual reality to blockchain and decentralized platforms, we examine the potential of these technologies to shape the future of music creation, distribution, and consumption. This chapter highlights the dynamic and ever-evolving relationship between music and technology and its impact on the soundtrack of humanity.

10

Chapter 10: Music and Culture

Music is an integral part of culture, reflecting and shaping the values, beliefs, and traditions of different societies. This chapter explores the relationship between music and culture, examining how music serves as a means of cultural expression and communication. We begin by exploring the role of music in traditional cultures, where it is often intertwined with rituals, ceremonies, and social practices.

We delve into the ways in which music reflects cultural identities and histories. From the indigenous music of Native American tribes to the classical traditions of European orchestras, we examine how different cultures use music to express their unique identities and preserve their heritage. The chapter also explores the role of music in cultural exchange and hybridization, where different musical traditions blend and influence each other.

The chapter also examines the impact of globalization on music and culture. The rise of global communication and digital technology has facilitated the spread of music across borders, leading to the emergence of new genres and styles. We explore the ways in which globalization has influenced musical practices and cultural identities, as well as the challenges and opportunities it presents.

Additionally, we look at the role of music in social and political movements, where it has been used to challenge oppression, promote social justice, and foster cultural solidarity. From the protest songs of the civil rights movement to the anthems of contemporary social movements, we examine how music serves as a powerful tool for social change. This chapter highlights the profound and multifaceted relationship between music and culture and its significance in the tapestry of human history.

11

Chapter 11: The Future of Music

As we look to the future, the landscape of music continues to evolve in response to technological advancements, cultural shifts, and global trends. This chapter explores the potential future of music, examining emerging trends and innovations that are shaping the next chapter of the soundtrack of humanity. We begin by exploring the impact of artificial intelligence on music creation and production.

We delve into the ways in which AI is being used to compose music, generate new sounds, and enhance music production. From AI-driven composition tools to machine learning algorithms that analyze and predict musical trends, we examine the potential of AI to revolutionize the music industry. The chapter also explores the ethical and creative implications of AI in music, including questions of authorship, originality, and the role of human creativity.

The chapter also examines the potential of virtual reality and augmented reality to transform music experiences. VR and AR technologies offer new ways for artists and audiences to engage with music, from immersive concert experiences to interactive music videos. We explore the possibilities and challenges of these technologies, as well as their potential to shape the future of music performance and consumption.

Additionally, we look at the role of blockchain and decentralized platforms in the music industry. These technologies offer new ways to distribute and monetize music, potentially disrupting traditional models of music production and distribution. We examine the implications of these developments for artists, listeners, and the music industry as a whole.

Finally, we consider the future of musical genres and styles. As the world becomes increasingly interconnected, new musical fusions and innovations continue to emerge. We explore the potential for cross-cultural collaboration and the ways in which diverse musical traditions will continue to inspire and influence each other. This chapter highlights the dynamic and ever-changing nature of music and its potential to shape the future of human experience.

12

Chapter 12: The Universal Language of Music

Music is often described as a universal language, transcending cultural, linguistic, and social barriers. This chapter explores the idea of music as a universal language and its significance in the human experience. We begin by examining the ways in which music connects people across different cultures and backgrounds, fostering understanding and empathy.

We delve into the concept of musical universals, which are elements of music that are found in diverse cultures around the world. By analyzing examples from various musical traditions, we see how certain rhythmic patterns, melodic structures, and harmonic intervals resonate across cultural boundaries. This exploration highlights the shared aspects of the human experience and the ways in which music reflects our common humanity.

The chapter also examines the role of music in promoting cross-cultural understanding and dialogue. From international music festivals to cross-cultural collaborations, we explore the ways in which music serves as a bridge between different cultures. By fostering cultural exchange and mutual appreciation, music can help to break down barriers and promote a sense of global community.

Additionally, we look at the therapeutic and healing potential of music as a universal language. Music therapy has been used to promote well-being and healing in diverse cultural contexts, highlighting its universal appeal and effectiveness. We explore the ways in which music can transcend cultural differences and support healing and resilience.

Finally, we reflect on the enduring power of music to connect us to our shared humanity. Whether through the primal beats of ancient drums or the sophisticated compositions of modern symphonies, music continues to resonate with us on a deep and fundamental level. Music has the ability to connect us to our past, inspire us in the present, and guide us into the future. This chapter celebrates the universality of music and its enduring power to bring people together.

13

Chapter 13: Music in Times of Crisis

In times of crisis, music has often served as a source of comfort, solidarity, and hope. This chapter explores the role of music during periods of social, political, and economic upheaval. We begin by examining historical examples of how music has been used to address and respond to crises, from wartime anthems to protest songs.

We delve into the ways in which music has provided solace and strength during difficult times. During wars, for example, music has been used to boost morale, provide emotional support, and foster a sense of unity among soldiers and civilians. From the stirring marches of World War I to the protest songs of the Vietnam War, we explore how music has been a powerful tool for coping with the hardships of conflict.

The chapter also examines the role of music in social and political movements. Protest songs have been used to challenge injustice, advocate for change, and mobilize communities. We explore the impact of iconic protest songs, such as "We Shall Overcome" during the civil rights movement and "Fight the Power" during the fight against systemic racism. These songs have become anthems of resistance and symbols of hope.

Additionally, we look at the ways in which music has been used to address economic crises and natural disasters. Benefit concerts, charity singles, and fundraising campaigns have mobilized musicians and communities to support relief efforts and raise awareness. From Live Aid to recent COVID-19 relief concerts, we see how music has the power to inspire collective action and provide support in times of need.

Finally, we reflect on the enduring resilience of humanity and the role of music in fostering hope and healing during crises. Music has the ability to provide comfort, offer a sense of normalcy, and remind us of our shared humanity. This chapter highlights the vital role of music in helping individuals and communities navigate challenging times.

14

Chapter 14: The Global Soundtrack

As we conclude our journey through the history and impact of music, we turn our attention to the global soundtrack that defines our contemporary world. This chapter explores the rich diversity of musical traditions and the ways in which they interact and influence each other in our increasingly interconnected world. We begin by examining the concept of world music and the ways in which different cultures contribute to the global musical landscape.

We delve into the unique musical traditions of various regions, from the rhythmic beats of Afrobeat in West Africa to the intricate melodies of Indian classical music. By exploring the distinctive characteristics of these traditions, we gain an appreciation for the cultural diversity and richness that define the global soundtrack. We also examine the ways in which these traditions have been influenced by and have influenced other musical genres, creating a dynamic and evolving musical tapestry.

The chapter also explores the role of globalization in shaping the global soundtrack. The rise of digital technology and global communication has facilitated the exchange of musical ideas and the emergence of new genres and styles. We examine the impact of cultural fusion and hybridization on the global musical landscape, as well as the ways in which artists and listeners navigate the complexities of cultural appropriation and appreciation.

Additionally, we look at the role of music in promoting cross-cultural

THE SOUNDTRACK OF HUMANITY, MUSIC, MIND, AND THE TAPESTRY OF HUMAN HISTORY

understanding and global solidarity. Music festivals, international collaborations, and cultural exchanges provide opportunities for artists and audiences to engage with diverse musical traditions and foster mutual appreciation. We explore the potential of music to break down barriers, challenge stereotypes, and promote a sense of global community.

Finally, we reflect on the future of the global soundtrack and the ways in which music will continue to evolve in response to cultural, technological, and social changes. As we look to the future, we celebrate the enduring power of music to connect us, inspire us, and enrich our lives. This chapter concludes our exploration of the soundtrack of humanity and its profound impact on the tapestry of human history.

The Soundtrack of Humanity: Music, Mind, and the Tapestry of Human History

Description:

Embark on an extraordinary journey through time with "The Soundtrack of Humanity," a captivating exploration of music's profound impact on human civilization. This enlightening book delves into the intricate relationship between music, the human mind, and the rich tapestry of our collective history.

From the earliest rhythms of ancient tribes to the complex compositions of modern symphonies, music has always been a powerful force in shaping human culture and experience. "The Soundtrack of Humanity" takes readers on a fascinating voyage, uncovering the origins of music and its evolution across diverse cultures and eras.

Discover the magic of melody and harmony, the driving pulse of rhythm, and the technological advancements that have transformed the way we create and enjoy music. Each chapter offers a deep dive into a specific aspect of music, from its emotional and cognitive impact to its role in social movements and cultural identity.

Explore how music has been a source of solace and strength in times of crisis, a tool for healing and well-being, and a universal language that transcends borders. Through vivid storytelling and insightful analysis, this book highlights the enduring power of music to connect us, inspire us, and

CHAPTER 14: THE GLOBAL SOUNDTRACK

enrich our lives.

"The Soundtrack of Humanity" is an essential read for anyone who has ever been moved by a melody or felt the heartbeat of a drum. It is a celebration of music's timeless significance and its ability to unite us all in a shared human experience.

www.ingramcontent.com/pod-product-compliance
Lightning Source LLC
LaVergne TN
LVHW020741090526
838202LV00057BA/6161